THE WILD GOOSE

POEMS

ALSO BY KEVIN GALLAGHER

POETRY

Isolate Flecks
Looking for Lake Texcoco
Gringo Guadalupe
Come Over and Help Us
LOOM
Radio Plays
The Apprentice from Drogheda
And Yet it Moves

EDITED WORK

spoKe: (2014- present, with Karina van Berkum)

Ceremonial Entries: the poetry of Joseph Deroche (with Martha Collins)

Greatest Hits: 10 years of compost *magazine* (with Margaret Bezucha)

compost: (1992–2003, with Margaret Bezucha, Anastasios Kozaitis, Margie Nicoll, Louis Pingatore, Christopher Seifert)

THE WILD GOOSE

KEVIN GALLAGHER

LP

Loom Press
Amesbury, Massachusetts
2022

Printed in the United States of America
First Edition

Design: Keith Finch
Cover: O'Reilly, John Boyle, *Athletics and Manly Sport*
(Boston Publishing Company, Boston 1890)
Printing: Versa Press
Typeface: Berkely Oldstyle and Dead Kansas

Loom Press
15 Atlantic View, Amesbury, MA 01913
www.loompress.com
info@loompress.com

for Robert P. Gallagher

Author's Note

The Wild Goose was a hand-made magazine written and edited by John Boyle O'Reilly aboard the Hougoumont, the last ship to transport British convicts to Australia. O'Reilly (1844-1890) was an Irish Fenian sentenced to life imprisonment for infiltrating the British army and attempted mutiny. He and his fellow editor and poet prisoners named the journal after the exiled "Wild Geese" Fenian soldiers of the Eighteenth Century. He escaped from Australia aboard a whaling ship and settled in Boston where he rose to become an editor of *The Pilot*, a noted poet, and abolitionist. O'Reilly is said to have been the favorite poet of President John F. Kennedy. There are few statues of poets in Boston: Phillis Wheatley, Edgar Allan Poe, and Robert Burns. There are two of John Boyle O'Reilly.

In a sense, these poems are also a little magazine conceived of and drafted in 2018 and 2019 while I was a poet-in-residence at the Heinrich Boll Cottage on Achill Island, County Mayo, Ireland. Boll visited frequently and for a time lived on Achill Island in the 1950s and 1960s. It is said that he wrote some of his major works there, including *The Clown* and, of course, *The Irish Journal*. Purchased in 2003, Boll's cottage is a residence for Irish and international poets and artists. My special thanks go to the sculptor John McHugh who coordinates the cottage, and to Kevin and Leslie Bowen, and John Mulrooney for telling me about this extraordinary place.

These pages include the sequence titled *The Journal of John Boyle O'Reilly: The Apprentice from Drogheda*. An earlier limited-edition version was published by Red Fox Press, Achill Island, in 2020. If you ever make it to Achill Island you must drive by the Boll cottage and then roll down the hill to visit the gallery at Red Fox Press on the Doogort cliffs overlooking the Atlantic Ocean. Thank you Frances Van Maele and Ham.

As in the O'Reilly sequence, the poems in this book engage the Irish landscape, the history, and myth that formed the identity of some of my ancestors until British colonialism and associated famine led them to Massachusetts. The book also snapshots Irish-American encounters in my life and pays special homage to "the Rose"—my late father Robert P. Gallagher—to whom this book is dedicated.

CONTENTS

The Wild Goose

Birth of a Nation

Eithlinn smelled love in the sea,
saw sex when she looked at the sun,

and when she rested her eyes at night,
she sensed love in her dreams.

Her father, Balor, made the De Danaan
pay up one third of all their grain,

one third of all their milk,
and one child of every three

to feed his greed and army.
A druid told him he would die

by the hand of his grandson,
so he locked up his only child,

Eithlinn, in a lonely tower
guarded by twelve warrior women

all sworn to never mention
or ever let Eithlinn see a man.

She heard songs come from the sea
that none of her guardians could make out.

Whenever she heard them she
felt birds beating their wings in her chest.

Too soon Eithlinn was fully grown,
mature, and beautiful.

She wanted her full breasts to be kissed.
She wanted to fill her empty womb.

She was so alone in her tower.
Balor wanted to feed his power

so he turned Eithlinn into a boy
and stole Cian's favorite cow.

Cian went to Birog, the she
druid who disguised Cian

as a woman and blew him
high off to Balor's island

where he landed safely
at the foot of Eithlinn's lonely tower.

Birog spelled the guardians to sleep
and Cian was to look for his cow--

but standing before him
was the most stunning woman

he had ever seen or dreamed of.
He turned right back into a man.

As Cian stared at her
Eithlinn's whole body went warm.

She now saw what she only heard.
She now had what she only dreamed of.

They each declared their love
for each other in the same breath

then gently took off the other's clothes
before they could breathe another.

He buried his face in her breasts
as she put him between her thighs

and sang a long slow psalm
of love up into the skies.

Cian wanted to live with her forever
but knew Balor would kill him.

Birog blew him another wind.
Cian left, but left behind a son.

BRES THE BEAUTIFUL (THE SATIRE OF CAIRBRE)

He can't expect to rule with a silver arm
even if losing his arm re-gained our land.

You are the man in the most perfect shape.
Put on that crown and we call you king.

You are a gifted master of love spells.
You are the ornament of your hosts.

You can drink all the milk of dune-hued line.
When I came to your court to sign these things

you locked me in a little dark cage
without a bed and with an empty hearth,

with just three dry cakes and a tiny plate.
Bres your prosperity is no more!

Three days of charred bulrush powder,
'joint to joint and sinew to sinew,

sinew and sinew and joint to joint.'
Nuada can point forward on his own.

Deirdre's Prophesy

I let out a shriek for you
before I was even born.

I saw a raven swoop
to drink the blood of a skinned calf.

The blood seeped across the snow
through my cell window.

You had black hair like that raven.
Your skin glowed like that snow.

Your cheeks were red as that blood
and I will love you forever.

You begged me to let you go
but I made you take me away

by threatening to take your honor.
You loved me too much anyway.

We fled to the purple valleys.
We loved the lochs and the mountains.

We were tricked into coming back.
My kind Conor made Eogan

drive his sword through your back.
Now I am stuck between two rams.

I leap from their chariot
and fall to follow you to the rocks.

LIR'S LETTER TO HIS CHILDREN

after Clannad

No matter where you go I will find you,
even if it takes me a thousand years.
I will do whatever I have to do.

I will go wherever I have to go.
I won't stop until I find you. Have no fear.
No matter where you go I will find you.

I know you are looking for me too.
I will be following your trail of tears.
I will do whatever I have to do.

My love for you is what carries me through.
My life is empty until you appear.
No matter where you go I will find you.

I hope that when I see you I will know.
Be sure to call out to me. I will hear.
I will do whatever I have to do.

I will go wherever I have to go.
Whenever I see swans I know you are near.
No matter where you go I will find you.
even if it takes me a thousand years.

St. Patrick

Our entire village was trying to raise
a marble flagstone to worship our lord

but the weight of the slab was much too great.
Hundreds of us were about to be crushed

but a huge man on a glowing white horse
galloped up and flung the marble away!

The stone was so heavy he fell from his horse.
In an instant the horse was gone. The giant stood

then withered into wrinkles and went blind
before our eyes. We bring him here to you.

St Patrick, we have seen a miracle!
Welcome to God's Kingdom, St. Patrick said.

'I am Osin from the Tir na nog,
son of Finn Mac Cumhaill. I scorn your King!'

THE HALF-BENT KNEE

Grace O'Malley and Queen Elizabeth, 1593

Her face was a mask of white powder and rouge.
Her nose was green hooked, like a Harridan's.

Her hair waved golden sun bars.
Her collar rang her head like castle walls.

Her dress was long and as light as gauze
but had more silver and gold than all Mayo.

Elizabeth held out her hand but Grace
was the taller one so the Queen raised her hand.

Grace needed a handkerchief. The Queen
pulled her lace-edged fine cambric from her pocket.

Grace used it then threw it in the fire.
That was for my pocket! said the startled Queen.

Knowing that she could easily be hanged,
Grace said back home we are cleaner than that.

Mass Rock, Achill Island

for Kevin and Leslie Bowen

We both worship the same God
but they don't like the way we do.
Since they write the rules
we are forbidden to pray to you.

A skiff slides in under the fog
and a 'beggar' leaps out with a bulky sleeve.
He roams the streets with an open hand, setting off
a bush telegram for we who believe.

So you roll fog down Croaghan
and give us all cover to set foot
over the hills then down to Keem
to step back up Croaghan again.

We Sweeneys, O'Malleys, Gallaghers,
(and our secret priest) rise to a hidden
Mass rock up Croughan Mountain.
The candid sun shines over the fog below.

The Atlantic wind behind us
is your organ playing fair.
There is no way they will know
we sing for Christ way out here.

Sheep bah like chanting monks
as the ocean claps on the shore.
The priest unsleeves a secret
crucifix, a cross, and our host.

We kneel on heather and moss
as the priest begs you to pray for us.
The high Cathedral cliffs
of Minuan pipe our voices high

above the fog for a quiet
song with you without them knowing.
As we take this bread, your life,
shadows of slow rolling fog

feel like flocks of angels
sent from you to comfort us
and cloak us from our troubles
as we hike back to Dooagh and even Keel.

BRITISH CLEARANCE SONG

What use can small farmers possibly be?
That lazy root that grows in lazy beds
is grown by you lazy people.
For every one of you I am charged a fee
but none of you pay anything to me.
It is time for me to set you free.
I won't be breeding paupers any more.
I clear you from your land and burn your roof.

I turn potato beds into pasture.
I hand the land back to Protestant Scots.
I weed out the idle and dishonest.
I sweep you to the embraces of death.
I cut down the exuberance of your tree.
If you dare survive, I bury you alive.

THE SKULLS OF SCHULL

for Catherine Moriarty Gallagher

Hugh's children made it
into the village
telling all who would listen
that for four whole days
they held father's hands
and begged him for food—
but father just stared at them
and didn't say anything back.

And, he is as cold as a flag.

Mother has been asleep
with little brother under the blanket.
Father covered them with
before Father took his nap.

My sister says they crawl with rats,
you can just make out his little legs.

May the good Lord avert
by his gracious interposition

the merited tokens of his displeasure
because there is no means to bury them.

All the Heavy Days are Over (Aleel's Grace)

The dead are staring at the ceilings
as they lie flat on their backs in bed
looking just as they did while screaming
aloud let in some bloody help.

The doors themselves became unscrewed
as Balor stopped winking his eye at them.
Balor knows they will never scream again.
The neighbors don't want to look that way.

They scurry like mice for crumbs all day
but slouch back home with nothing to show
but stories of tricky demons that glow
without leaving any shadows behind.

Instead they plant tiny seeds in your mind.
Your apron can hold this crock of gold.
All you need to do is sell out your soul.
I tried to trade my soul for nothing

but the demons knew my soul wasn't mine
to give but belonged to Cathleen alone.
The burden in her eyes had broken my wits.
The demon replied I won't touch it, begone!

But trading for Cathleen made him smile
as he laid down bags of gold in heaps
for those cheap little souls she saved.
Cathleen had the wood for a future of fire.

Now she has left the body's colored pride.
She gazes at me with a swallow's grace.
She strengthens me to sing to the dancers
who don't know the burdens of the world—

as angels and demons clash with words
and thunder pounds on lightning swords.
The dancer's stage, the platform of her peace.
Bless her with prayers each time you eat.

EMIGRANT SONG

for Hugh Gallagher

I had to bid
a forever farewell

to my native land
of Donegal.

It was never my choice
to leave the place.

Our landlord torched our roof
and took our land.

Leaving was a matter
of life or death.

It's hard to say good-bye
but I leave you

for the jobs in the factories
with the looms

for the great beef
served on China plates

for mutton and Cuban
gin in crystal

for that's much better
than the grub back home

of a cup of milk
and a lumper spud.

COFFIN SHIP

One pound of bread
for each adult.

A half pound
if under fourteen.

One third if
younger than 7.

The medicine chest,
a jar of castor oil,

epsom salts,
laudanum, and hartshorn

all for 110 souls
and as many bodies.

We have never seen
a ship or the sea.

We are going
but don't know where.

Roll on thou dark
and deep blue ocean, roll.

For evening prayers
in the hold

we are divided
into two molds:

Irish speakers
and those who don't.

We shall not be afraid
for terror by night,

nor the arrow of day,
nor the sickness

that destroys the way
we sing at the sea.

Red and purple spots
turn to putrid sores.

Water for God's sake
some water please.

The dead
go overboard

in swollen faces
like small deformed casks.

Shrouded corpses
lowered into the ocean
on old sails are floating tombs.

The Journal of
John Boyle O'Reilly

THE APPRENTICE FROM DROGHEDA

1865

The world is small when the enemy is loose.
I'll rest when they have nooses on their necks.
I know what I have been born here to do.

I won't be a serf on our land they took.
I won't just stand here as we starve to death.
The world is small when the enemy is loose.

We are losing our faith, our lives, our food.
The ugly truth is they might hang me first.
But now I know what I am here to do:

to fight for freedom and independence too.
I'll kill undercover in a British vest.
The world is shrinking and the enemy is loose,

a silent voice won't do anyone good.
Life is your chance to make your own events.
I know what it is that I have to do

even if it means I will meet my doom.
At least I will die in the pursuit of truth.

The world is shrinking and the enemy is loose.
Now I know what I was born here to do.

So Help Us God

I sing Irish songs in a British coat.
Eighty others of the Prince's Hussars

march for the Crown but whistle the same tunes.
We swear allegiance to the Republic.

We will yield to our officer's commands.
We will take arms at a moment's notice.

We copy defense plans. We have gate keys.
We have maps of military strategy.

We are the true soldiers of Liberty.
Give us a signal for the mutiny!

Oh that signal never came. England
has not been asleep. You found the names

of fifteen thousand of us Fenians.
It was we who had plotted in our sleep.

MY TURN WILL COME NEXT

I was waiting at our barrack's window
watching our troops approach at Island Bridge.

We were to snip the tendons in the hind legs
of the Dragoon's horses with the signal.

But I tensed right up and my spine went cold
as the military police seized some of us

and kept entering the parade for more.
One by one each of us was singled out

and herded into the garrison guard house.
I turned from the window. I sat in bed.

I wondered how anyone could have known.
I said to myself my turn will come next.

A heavy fist pounded the barrack's door.
I stood up and left without a word.

DRUMMING OUT

I was sentenced to life in prison
starting with six months of solitary confinement.

Parades of troops assembled in the square
in their dark blue cloth and their heavy braid

with fife and drums behind their marching feet.
All for me! Several thousand 10th Dragoon Guards,

the 3rd and 75th Regiments,
the 85th Light Infantry and a big brass band.

I also wore their cloth and their heavy braid.
While the large crowds stood still at attention,

you stripped the cloth from me piece by piece,
you clothed me in a woolen convict dress,

you shackled me in chains, you marched me through the streets
where all of Dublin could see me in my pride.

Dartmor

1867

Dartmor was guarded by a wrap of mist
on top of a hill with a very steep slope,

giant iron rails some fifteen feet tall,
and endless marshland in the fog below.

You bound my ankles like a shackled beast.
You split my skin with brutal whips and clubs.

My cell was seven feet long, four feet wide,
and barely seven feet to the ceiling.

I saw through a two-inch hole in my door.
I could see the sun in the corridor.

Like the French in the Napoleonic wars
and Americans in the War of 1812,

my life would be digging drainage ditches.
Until, of course, I could make my escape.

ESCAPE

I slid from the drains and hid in the fog
until my fellow prisoners were taken

back up the hill—then I ran for the coast.
I heard the prison bells when the guards learned

there was no one to return to my cell.
I didn't eat, drink, or sleep at all.

I was too scared to beg or stop.
Briars and branches ripped my clothes off.

I heard their dogs and ran for a river.
I was a white fright running through the night.

I dipped in slowly without a ripple.
I collapsed unconscious and you caught me.

Well I beat you for two days and two nights.
Your biggest mistake was not hanging me.

HELL OR THE *HOUGOUMONT*

Your footsteps in the corridor again.
Your keys rattled and my door opened up.

Your guards put double irons on my arms
then chained us together in bright new steel.

Get up, O'Reilly, you pushed and said,
on your way Irishman. You are leaving!

We didn't look into each other's eyes.
We learned to know what the other was thinking

without having to look or even speak.
You were shipping me to Australia

on the *Hougoumont*—a blood-stained hellship
manned with brazen faces and sloppy sailor suits.

At that point some prisoners gave up their hope.
Yet I had another chance to escape.

1867

We were too much for England's little prisons.
We the mad, sick, and reeking overflow

walking in line on deck for a flogging.
Murderers, rapists, thieves, and my politics.

The first thing they did was knock off my chains
and order me to go down below deck.

There were three hundred of us without shadows
cast by lamps under the forward hold.

We welcomed each other with loud
laughter curses of the most evil fear.

A warm stranger gripped my arm and whispered
come O'Reilly we are waiting for you.

He led me through a small door amidships
to the space where we waitied to be slaves.

THE TIMES OF LONDON

October 10, 1867

Quite a large count of turbulent spirits
are among the miscreants aboard ship.

We know what Fenian folly will dare.
They left their country for their country's good,

but a scene of carnage on the ocean
and resistance to our lawful authority

is within the range of possibility
when mixing mad criminals with the Irish.

These rowdies consider themselves martyrs
and constitute three-fourths of the living

beings who are cooped in that convict ship.
Panic has taken Australian settlers

demanding that the ship be promptly seized
before rape and pillage flow from the sea.

Prisoner 9843

After years of cutting and blasting roads
my job was to hack the jungle to death.

Black skinned Bush men moved all around us,
their chiefs wore hammered breastplates of pure gold.

Not one single white man ever found an ounce
but these Australians would never give up.

Riveted to thirty pounds of iron,
separated from my compatriots,

you gave me an axe and taught me to swing.
I looked at the army of mahogany

lit up by thousands of white cockatees
motionless under the blue copper sky.

My sweat would sting and my axe would ring,
and those giants of a lost age fell down.

THE WARDEN'S DAUGHTER

13 March, 1868

Do you love me, she said, when the skies are blue,
and we walk where the stream always glistens?

I told her and told her my love was true.
She listened and smiled and smiled and listened.

Do you love me she said when days are drear?
And her eyes searched mine with patient yearning.

Reviewing those words so dear I kissed you.
You kissed me and cried, you were slowly learning

that we could never live a life of love
though we love each other up to our ears.

If your father found out what we were full of
neither of us would see another year.

In another life we will love again.
Love robs life of pleasure and death of pain.

THE VIGILANT

There's a tide in the affairs of men
that taken at the flood leads to fortune.

I would rather ride the tide to death
than to stay here in shackles half alive.

My love made me a pair of Freeman's boots.
Father Max fixed it that I'd be snuck out.

We pulled eight hours within two miles of her.
She was a golden angel in the sun.

Her wings the spreading sails, were wide open.
We flagged my white shirt on top of an oar

and hailed enough to be heard on board
but *The Vigilant* turned off course.

The captain took our money and gave his word.
We took a whole day to get back to shore.

Letter from Father McCabe

2 March 1869

The ship *Gazelle* will sail off tomorrow.
Her Captain, Gifford, knows where you are.

She will put in to the coast and take you.
I paid ten pounds but she says they are for you.

You will need the money in America.
There is one unpleasantry to mention.

One of the convicts found out our plan.
He threatens the truth unless he comes too.

I gave him safe conduct to your hideout.
He is the worst prisoner in the *Vasse*.

The whole country is searching for you two.
I'm sorry this is how it has to be.

Fair winds and safe voyage to your new home.
Remember me in your prayers—FATHER MAC.

ABSCONDER

to the attention of all British Colonies, 1869

John Boyle O'Reilly   registered No.
9843   imperial convict

arrived in the colony   per convict ship
Hougoumont   in 1868

sentenced to twenty years   9th July
1866.   Description   —   healthy

appearance   present age   25 years
5 feet 7 ½ inches

high   black hair   brown eyes   dark
complexion   and convicted   Irishman.

Dangerous   conniving   untrustworthy
revolutionary   against the crown.

Absconded from Convict Road Party
Bunbury,   18th of February.

SONNET TO THE SUN

The Gazelle was a New Bedford whaler
two and a half years out from its home port.

Took me as far as the Cape of Good Hope.
There I boarded *The Sapphire,* from Boston,

and sailed all the way to Liverpool.
I stepped on your shore with the name John Soule.

No one expected Prisoner 9843
to be under their nose on a cargo ship.

We passed Ireland as we sailed westward.
The sun's rays of golden glory flowed down

on my old home on the hill, wood and river
like God's pity on Ireland's face.

Thank you for shining the light on the same
heaven of long ago, once more, for me.

Cooper Institute, Welcome Speech

16 December, 1869

I stood on the platform and I looked out
at two thousand people cheering my name.

As the tears bubbled around my eyes
you were standing on your feet screaming 'hero'

hoping I would lift up all your souls.
I told them my story straight from my heart.

I spoke of my fight for Irish freedom.
I spoke of sacrifice for my country-men.

I spoke of my horrors in the prisons.
I spoke of sympathy and good will.

I want to be an American.
My first task here is citizenship.

I have been following all the signs.
Great men grow greater by the lapse of time.

HELP WANTED

Boston 1870

Positively No Irish need apply?
We were half-starved and penniless

farmers without any tools for the city.
Most of the us went working on the wharfs.

Women made factory shoes or sewed from home.
We had our will, our music, and our GOD,

but many wondered why we traveled here.
I had worked as a printer, a soldier,

a poet, a sailor. I dug ditches.
I was a whale boat man, a convict,

courier, and mahogany sawyer.
For those vacancies I'd had enough.

I want to be a newspaper man.
My only weapon will be my pen.

THE FIGHT AT TROUT RIVER

13 June 1870

I gave my life to you and you saved me
but today I abandon your cause.

To attack Britain via Canada
was hopelessly wrong and miserably flawed,

and almost became our mass suicide.
Fenianism has lost its power.

We have done all the evil we can do.
We kept thousands away from their homes.

We have caused the death of several brave men
for this wild and futile enterprise.

With you I do no good for Ireland.
I am not saying I am your enemy.

I wish you the success you are aiming for.
This is not the way for me to be free.

Boston Pilot

23 July 1870

3000 Orangemen marched for the Boyne
'To hell with the Pope! To hell with the Pope!'

Fenians returned with a pistol shot,
four Irish dead on the streets of New York.

Why must we carry our cursed island feuds
to disturb the peace of these citizens?

We are all aliens from a petty island
in the eyes of our fellow Americans. Here

the Orange have as much right to parade
as a Fenian regiment in green.

Both parties are to be blamed and condemned,
yes both the Fenian and the Orangemen.

America has had enough of us now.
There is only one flag for us to hold.

FREEDOM OF THE PRESS

Boston Club, July 1872

I see the yellow paper and the small page
as a twenty-four hour photograph--

of a mysterious river of time
that is flowing past us forever.

Never moving in straight or simple lines,
paragraphs are mosaics of our lives.

We have more tales of joy and suffering,
ambition and defeat, and villainy and virtue

than all the greatest books ever written.
We roll them up to light a fire

or set them free in the skies with the gulls.
I resign all of my prejudices.

I call you all my fellow citizens,
there still remains a mountain to be moved.

We can succeed where our forerunners failed
or take them home wrapping up fish and chips.

Faneuil Hall

1885

We don't have "colored peoples waiting rooms"
but I know many hotels in Boston

where you would say all your rooms are filled
if any one of them asked for a room.

You can't legislate conceit out of white people.
This outrage is higher than any law.

The black man is the only American
who has written new songs and new music.

The black man is the most spiritual.
He worships with his soul and without his mind.

The black man will bring great poets, painters,
and great fashioners of God's beautiful shapes

in clay, in marble, and in harmony.
I shall be counted in with the black man.

PRIVATE GAR QUOTE

Are you conscious
of the consequence

of going to a profane
irreligious

pagan country
of gross materialism

where the devil himself
holds sway with a lust

that everyone is
shamelessly indulged in?

Don't you think
maybe you should stick it out?

Shamelessly, sir,
shamelessly I submit.

Then strike out on your own
once you find your feet.

Don't keep looking back
over your shoulder.

Be one hundred percent
American.

A back yard,
a great big cherry tree,

snow at Christmas,
the dog in the parlor.

Squirrels and night owls,
all so God awful

because you won't
have me to share it with.

THE DEATH OF A TWO-TOILET IRISHMAN

Martin Faherty, 1915-2012

"Don't mourn these men thank God they were alive"
Patton said in a speech at Copley Square.

His father dead, O'Higgins too, Churchill's
gold mistake also left the subjects screwed.

His mother came to "Biddy" on Beacon Hill
and Marty worked ships at Fore River until

war called him to fight with Patton's Super Sixth.
He found himself at the Battle of the Bulge.

He broke the clock for good at Buchenwald.
Skeletons with white skin coats and some hope

tried to lift their heroes on their shoulders,
but they were all at the end of their ropes.

The "No Irish Need Apply" signs were gone
when he came back. He got himself a job

at First National as a meat-cutter.
He met Mary, had a girl and two boys.

He bought the family into a triple-decker
on Asticou Street in Jamaica Plain.

Mary answered an ad when the kids grew
that simply read "secretary needed."

She worked thirteen championships for Red
while Marty toasted the television set.

He saved up to open Walk Hill Market
and become a two-toilet Irishman

in West Roxbury and later the Cape.
There he loved family, history, the *Quarterdeck*.

He declares all your power to the next,
your mighty acts to all who are to come.

THOSE SUMMER SATURDAYS

Saturdays too my dad woke up early.
Put on his grass-stained Sperry Topsiders,

his green Bermudas with paint stains and whales,
then took the entire day to mow the lawn.

He'd snap open and fire up his Zippo
then mow two perfect rows with a Salem

Menthol 100 shrinking from his mouth.
Time to take a break for a Miller Lite,

to turn up Ken Coleman for the Sox score
to shout it out for everyone to know.

He'd save the empty cans to be redeemed
then light another butt for two more rows.

One lawn, three packs, and a case in a day.
And what did I know? What did I know?

HOME RUN

Dad comes home in our only aqua blue
nineteen seventy-seven Vega coupe.

I run to stop him in the driveway.
I raise my fist with a golden glove,

holding it high like a liberty torch—
my hat and ball tucked under my shoulder.

Dad smiles as his thumbs shoot up over the wheel.
I lower my arm and let him go by.

He comes out in his work T-shirt and slacks,
flips open his Zippo lighter and lights up

a Salem Menthol 100, snaps
open a Miller Light, grabs a bat,

and starts cracking me pop flies.
"Who is he?" Dad would scream when I caught one.

I'd scream and throw back Rico Petrocelli!
Fred Lynn! Dewey! Yaz! Boomer! Jim Rice.

His cigarette became a firefly
in the night. The pop flies, bats in flight.

MARTIN LUTHER KING DAY MASSACRE

Austin, Texas, 1992

I.

A small parade of long white school buses
ascended up to the capitol steps.

A procession of white cone-headed capes
came out in single file, even some kids.

Protest against Martin Luther King Day.
The National Guard had their plastic shields,

their holsters, packed guns, and rubber bullets,
and all of them were wearing shades.

The Guard formed a layer between the Klan
and a thousand protestors protesting the protest.

Each side started screaming at the other
until the thousand broke out with a song:

"If you're happy and you know it moon the Klan,"
their bare butts read "KKK go away!"

II.

I put two quarters into a pay phone
to describe the crazy scene to my dad.

Even up north they had to work that day.
My dad's receptionist picked up the line,

surprised it was me on the other end.
Your father hasn't worked here in three months.

I didn't know what to say. I didn't.
I hung up as she repeated my name.

He hid this from me so I wouldn't worry.
After 30 years at Pittsburgh Plate Glass,

Dad was thrown out on the street on his ass
then swung from job to job that couldn't last.

Too old for them. Not enough new skills.
He told me he wanted to kill himself.

Mac Rebennack Reunion

June 6, 2019

My pop is front row
heeling in Peds

that pad his Docksiders.
Under a navy short-sleeved Lacoste

his salmon Bermudas
go all the way to his knee

belted by a blue row of green crickets
held by two gold rings.

He grips a Foster Lager oil can.
He angles a Salem Menthol 100.

The swamp has been drained
for the day but Heaven

will be a holy place tonight
as Dr. John reunites

w/ Professor Longhair
whistling Big Chief

and playing two pianos
in a jean jacket

goggles
and a purple velvet suit.

The snake on the cane
is finally alive.

The skull on the piano
can finally smile.

THE VALHALLA

1984

We had close to seven tons of mail-order
Weapons delivered by UPS.

We purchased them through ads in *Shotgun News*
by calling the 1-800 number.

We ordered ammunition cans, weapons,
training manuals, nylon rifle clips,

piles of M-16 magazines,
and rifle bags to hide them in the bogs.

We bought rocket warheads, anti-aircraft,
and 20,000 rounds home delivery special.

But the handguns, the rifles, and shotguns,
we stole those the old-fashioned way.

We packed all this in a couple of U-Hauls,
then drove the trucks up to Gloucester Harbor.

Twenty tons of ice was loaded below
one hundred pounds of squid, seven thousand

pounds of mackerel bait, and thirty
miles of long-line on an eight-foot spool

with all the weapons in the engine room
into the slavery of the Atlantic.

We cut the engine and pretended to fish
off Sable Island. On the radar

a hurricane hit off the Flemish Cap.
We made fourteen trips in our dinghy.

As we hit against the walls of the sea
we filled the *Marita Anna* with guns,

but the ship had been overcome by rats.
The Navy nailed us at Porcupine Banks.

Gay Parade

15 March 1992

We hate you
on West Broadway!

Get out of Southie
you bunch of fags!

God hates fags
I hope you all die

of AIDS you homos!
God created

Adam and Eve
Not Adam and Steve!

30 or 40 fucking goons
with 20 working teeth

among them don't
speak for all of us.

Happy St. Patrick's Day
and welcome to Southie!

Some waved back.

WELCOME BACK

You don't know how to pronounce your own name.
You hardly even know where you're from.

You parachute in here and blow the tires
off our rent-a-cars on our narrow roads.

I charge you twice as much for the replacements
in part because I know you have insurance,

in part because it just pisses me off
that part of you is so scared to be home.

Where were you on Easter, 1916?
You think being Irish is parading

your drunken face off on St. Patrick's Day
and drinking Black-and-Tans in Boston pubs?

We know you're never coming back for good.
If you did you wouldn't be understood.

BLACKSOD BAY

Achill 2019

The full moon
unfolds a thin sail

of light,
a gauze dress opening

over the cove.
The stars

sift through
as grains of salt,

echoed below
by tiny white boats,

sleeping white sheep,
and our white-washed cottages.

Our old stone homes
are faint in the shadows.

DOOKINELLA CHURCH OF OUR LADY
OF THE ASSUMPTION

we obeyed   the speed limit   on the way
to church   we saw   that the leaves were changing

we noted   which houses   needed painting
we pointed out   two hawks flying over

we did not   talk about   the horrors
that are happening   in our church   and state

we didn't have room   in our day   for hate
we pulled   into the parking lot   we waved

to our friends   already filling   inside
fairly quietly   and lining   in our pews

we sang psalms   looking sideways   at our priest

we were set free   when we got on our knees
we prayed for god   we prayed for god

Belfast Cab

Whitey Bulger would be shot bloody dead
or paraded through the streets a hero

depending on which side of the road I drop ya,
my Belfast cabby respectfully said

after I told him I was from Boston.
Is the fucking bastard still alive or in jail?

You know you could tell that a building
was going to blow up when the windows

would shatter all over the street before
the power of exploding brick would pop

and bang so loud you would cover your ears
right after you made sure you closed your eyes.

This ain't about no little skirmish at a parade.
This is about being dead or alive.

DRIVE-IN JESUS

Portrush Drive-in Church, Northern Ireland

Don't even think about driving through town
on a Sunday, you'll never get through.

The people parade in from every town around,
idling in single file, billowing incense

from their exhaust pipes as the altar boys
glide by singing psalms on their roller skates,

making sure everyone rests in peace.
Folks drive up to the microphone teller,

say an "Our Father," ten "Hail Mary's"
then they turn on A.M. 1360

playing "Glory to God in the Highest"
until they get to the drive-up window.

The teller pushes out her metal box,
parishioners put money in for the poor.

The teller reels in the cash, then pushes
it back with a host and a cup of wine.

They eat from his flesh, they drink from his blood,
click their seat belts back, then sign the cross.

The Rose in the Elysian Fields

CAIRBRE:

Your cackling riddles make the cave walls shake
but I'm not scared to beg to see his face.

I'll drink as many spirits as it takes
so I can bathe inside his memory.

I just want to lie in my father's shade
then read him the poem I wrote for him.

SIBYL:

I'm not asking you to build a temple
but you must show me a little respect

before I spring the underworld for you.
Don't you go thinking it is that easy.

You better get down on your knees and pray
you don't get so taken you don't come back.

The door isn't just going to swing open.
If it does, you won't like how it slams shut.

CAIRBRE:

I'll do anything. Name my sacrifice.
I will do whatever you want me to.

I will empty my bank account for you
or wash your dishes for the rest of my life.

SIBYL:

Hold your money. I was just testing you.
In some ways I am just a gatekeeper.

But now it's time to down your elixirs.
My door is open for one day and one night.

You can see him once before forever.
It is easy to get drunk and pass out,

but it's hard to wake up and see the light.
You have to go out and buy a gold leaf

bracelet and give it to my friend Sharon.
If Sharon likes it, she will let you cross.

SIBYL:

You must also visit the grave of Monch
who lives in a box right next to your father.

He was only in his early twenties
when he left and no one can see him now.

His parents have gone. His friends have left.
His name wasn't said at your reunion.

Only the birds and the weeds visit his stone.
You know he could have easily been you.

CAIRBRE:

Hey Dad. Monch never has any money
please slip him a butt and a couple bucks

when you can. He will never pay you back
but he is always fun to have around

and you two have the same taste in music.
He has plenty Mark, you'll be helping him.

He found his way to the dove gallery,
bought the gold-leaf bracelet in the window,
and the owner replaced it right away.

Dove owner:

Don't ever come in here so drunk again!

Cairbre:

Sorry. This is the only way to go.

Cairbre (now at Sharon's):

My friend suggested I give you this gift.

Sharon:

Thanks. I'll add it to my collection
then I'll take you across the Acheron.

Cairbre:

There is nothing I would rather do.
I am forever indebted to you.

Sharon:

Well. I hope you brought something for the dog.

Cairbre:

Don't worry I brought a thing or two.
But why do I feel like I'm surrounded?

Sharon:

There's a crowd of souls who beg to come too.

CAIRBRE:

I feel the memories of images
and people I can't stand all around me,

people that I haven't seen in a long time.
Kids that used to drive me crazy at school,

the bosses I hated to work for,
but I can see some old friends too.

I guess I am starting to feel this booze.
I swear I can reach out and grab the truth.

SHARON:

Don't worry. They can't pray for what they did.
They have not been called to the river bank.

Follow me now to death's deepest regions.
I am moved by how devoted you are—

even though you act like a stupid drunk
and groan the timbers off my leaky boat.

GERBER (GROWLING):

The reason why they say this is the bank
of the river that no one comes back across
is that I kill you the minute you step
off that ferry and on to my shore.

CAIRBRE:

But Gerber I brought you a drink we call
'nectar from the gods! It widens your chest

and helps you sing and scream at the same time--
so loud no one will ever leave the boat.

Heal. Let me come over and fill your bowl.
I came here to lie in my father's shade.

GERBER:

You better not be playing tricks on me.
I'm thirsty for new ways to scare your souls.

Try anything and I'll claw you to pieces.

SHARON:

I have to admit you're surprising me
but look around my friend. You are far from free.

PRISONER'S SONG (FROM THE WINDOWS OF TARTARUS):

I regret it now but I blew out my light
because I thought my life was a bore.
I didn't realize that life was so bright.

I'm surrounded by walls of infinite height
and the sage application of the toll.
I regret it that I blew out my light.

I rage against the dying of my life
knowing that no one will ever hear my call.
I didn't realize that life was so bright.

Death doesn't have the appeal that it might.
Death just put me under the God's control.
I regret it that I blew out my light.

If I could try again I'd do it right
but I can't try because I lost my soul.
I didn't realize my future was so bright.

There isn't another future in sight
for me so I live to blacken this hole.
I regret it that I blew out the light
I didn't see that the future was so bright.

Rose:

You don't have to go down that road my son.
Come here to the fields of Elysium.

See past those prisons, come under the sun
and the stars that can only be found here.

This is a world that is as pure as life.
Yes, at last. Are you here for me at last?

I can't believe I am seeing your face
and you are standing right in front of me.

I have always known your sense of right
would win and keep you coming to this end.

I am at peace with death but count the days.
Let me hear you talk. I'll talk to you too.

Cairbre:

I just came to read you the poem I wrote
after mom called me up to say you died.

CAIRBRE:

You can't be dead for the rest of my life.
I do not know how to live without you.
I can't want to see you until I die

but I can't make a rush for the other side.
I have a whole life that I have to do.
You can't be dead for the rest of my life.

I'm so afraid I will run out of time
but I don't have any time to lose.
I cannot wait to see you until I die.

When you aren't with me my life is a lie
and there is no such thing as the truth.
You can't be dead for the rest of my life.

The rest of my life is too long a line
and I wouldn't have anything to prove.
You can't be dead for the rest of my life.
I cannot wait to see you until I die.

ROSE:

You don't really want to know how I died.
The Courant said death by complications

due to several years of emphysema,
went on to talk about my wife and kids,

what I did for a living, my place of birth,
where to find the wake, where to send flowers.

Sure I smoked three packs of Salem Menthol
100s every day for fifty years.

I was blaring the Red Sox on TV
and loading the dishwasher while your mom watched

her thing downstairs even louder than mine.
I banged my shin on the dishwasher's jaw

and started to bleed. I called her name
loud and again until the ambulance came.

ROSE:

Do not try to hold me. You can't hold on.
I am a dream on wings between your hands.

My generation played our part then passed.
Your generation passed on your turn.

Do not worry, it is not your fault.
Do not worry about your life or mine.

There are more to come from these blessed fields.
The souls are floating back to the light

to grow into bodies and save the world.
They return with winged shoes and silver hounds

to pound the enemy and set us free
into a place of love and purity

erased from the horror, torture, and the war—
where all of us can live or rest in peace.

A Note on the Author

Kevin Gallagher is a poet, publisher, and political economist living in Greater Boston, USA, with his wife Kelly, kids Theo and Estelle, and Rexroth the family dog. His recent books are *Loom, Radio Plays,* and *And Yet it Moves.* He edits *spoKe,* a Boston-based annual of poetry and poetics and works as a professor of global development policy at Boston University. For ten years he co-edited *compost* magazine with collaborators around Boston.